Taffy wagged her tail excitedly, her fur fluffing up. She knew they were going on an adventure when her family started packing the car.

She barked happily, her eyes sparkling with excitement. She couldn't wait to start the drive to Grandma's house.

Taffy enjoyed the car ride with the wind in her ears. She watched in wonder as the scenery changed along the way.

When they stopped at the beach Taffy jumped out and ran along the shore. She felt the soft wet sand on her paws and sniffed the fresh sea air.

Taffy noticed a strange
star-shaped creature on the sand.
It was a starfish, a new friend
for Taffy. She smelled it
carefully, being sure
not to get too close.

The starfish moved slowly along the sand. Taffy followed them at a safe distance. She loved their shape and color.

Taffy's family called her back to the car as the sky turned orange. She said goodbye to her new friends the birds and starfish.

Taffy looked out the window as the breeze ruffling her fur. Her heart was full of joy. She promised to return to the beach soon.

They decided to take a hike in the forest. Taffy eagerly jumped out of the car.

The forest path led them to a
beautiful mountainside.
Taffy was amazed by the
height of the mountains.

They came to a stream and
Taffy danced through the
water. She smelled the pine
trees and cool mountain air.

Taffy saw a field of wildflowers
next to the stream. She ran
through the field happily,
scattering the butterflies
and flowers.

The hike continued to a
sparkling waterfall. A friendly
squirrel sat next to Taffy,
it's nose twitching as it
said hello.

Taffy loved the mountains, fields and waterfalls. She wagged her tail at each new sight and sound.

As she jumped back into the
car, Taffy thought of all the
new sights and smells she
had experienced.

Finally they arrived at Grandma's house! Taffy ran to the garden, her tail wagging with joy. Grandma greeted her with big hugs and kisses.

At the end of the day Taffy
rested as she thought about her
wonderful day of adventure with
her family. She slept dreaming
of chasing butterflies.

The End